TURNING POINTS IN U.S. HISTORY
DUST BOWL

by Veronica B. Wilkins

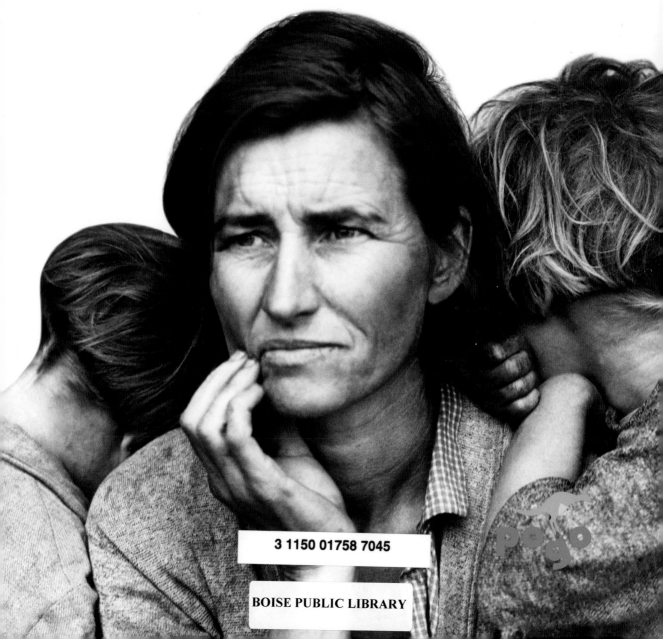

Ideas for Parents and Teachers

Pogo Books let children practice reading informational text while introducing them to nonfiction features such as headings, labels, sidebars, maps, and diagrams, as well as a table of contents, glossary, and index.

Carefully leveled text with a strong photo match offers early fluent readers the support they need to succeed.

Before Reading

- "Walk" through the book and point out the various nonfiction features. Ask the student what purpose each feature serves.
- Look at the glossary together. Read and discuss the words.

Read the Book

- Have the child read the book independently.
- Invite him or her to list questions that arise from reading.

After Reading

- Discuss the child's questions. Talk about how he or she might find answers to those questions.
- Prompt the child to think more. Ask: The Dust Bowl caused many people to leave their homes. How do you think that felt?

Pogo Books are published by Jump!
5357 Penn Avenue South
Minneapolis, MN 55419
www.jumplibrary.com

Library of Congress Cataloging-in-Publication Data

Names: Wilkins, Veronica B., 1994- author.
Title: Dust Bowl / Veronica B. Wilkins.
Description: Minneapolis, MN : Jump!, Inc., [2020]
Series: Turning points in U.S. history | Includes index.
Audience: Ages 7-10.
Identifiers: LCCN 2019020736
ISBN 9781645271376 (ebook)
ISBN 9781645271352 (hardcover : alk. paper)
ISBN 9781645271369 (pbk. : alk. paper)
Subjects: LCSH: Dust Bowl Era, 1931-1939 Juvenile literature. | Dust storms Great Plains History 20th century Juvenile literature. | Droughts Great Plains History 20th century Juvenile literature. | Farmers Great Plains History 20th century Juvenile literature. | Migrant labor Great Plains History 20th century Juvenile literature. | Farm life Great Plains History 20th century Juvenile literature. | Great Plains Social conditions 20th century Juvenile literature. | Depressions 1929 Great Plains Juvenile literature.
Classification: LCC F595 .W697 2020 | DDC 973.917 dc23
LC record available at https://lccn.loc.gov/2019020736

Editor: Susanne Bushman
Designer: Jenna Casura

Photo Credits: Everett Historical/Shutterstock, cover, 4, 16; Dorothea Lange/Farm Security Administration/Office of War Information Black-and-White Negatives/Library of Congress, 1, 3, 6-7, 14-15; Farm Security Administration/Office of War Information Black-and-White Negatives/Library of Congress, 5; Walker Evans/Farm Security Administration/Office of War Information Black-and-White Negatives/Library of Congress, 8-9; D. L. Kernodle/Farm Security Administration/Office of War Information Black-and-White Negatives/Library of Congress, 10-11; Bert Garai/Keystone/Hulton Archive/Getty, 12; Photo12/Universal Images Group/Getty, 13; Danita Delimont/Alamy, 17; Arthur Rothstein/Farm Security Administration/Office of War Information Black-and-White Negatives/Library of Congress, 18-19, 23; Elenathewise/iStock, 20-21.

Printed in the United States of America at Corporate Graphics in North Mankato, Minnesota.

TABLE OF CONTENTS

CHAPTER 1
Blowing Dust 4

CHAPTER 2
Farmers on the Move 12

CHAPTER 3
End of the Dust Bowl 16

QUICK FACTS & TOOLS
Timeline 22
Glossary 23
Index 24
To Learn More 24

CHAPTER 1

BLOWING DUST

The year was 1931. A dark cloud appeared in Oklahoma. But it wasn't rain. A giant dust storm blew dirt and dust across the **Great Plains**. The storm was so great that it blocked out the sun!

dust storm

Many dust storms damaged this area between 1931 and 1939. They ruined farmlands. Dust covered entire homes. This time is called the Dust Bowl. The area of the Great Plains that was hit hardest is also known as the Dust Bowl.

In the late 1800s, farmers turned grasslands in the Great Plains to farmland. They farmed the same land many times. Farmers **plowed** the soil too much. They let their **livestock** eat so much of the grass that it damaged the land.

Farmers plowed even more grasslands in 1929 and 1930. Why? The country entered the **Great Depression**. People across the country were poor. Farmers needed to grow more **crops** to make enough money.

plowing

eroded
soil

A **drought** began in 1930. The crops could not grow without rain. Their roots had held soil in place. Without the plants and their roots, soil began to **erode**.

DID YOU KNOW?

On May 11, 1934, dust from the Great Plains reached the Statue of Liberty in New York. It had blown almost 1,500 miles (2,414 kilometers)!

Dust storms began in 1931. In 1932, there were 14. In 1933, 38 more took place. The worst was on a Sunday in 1935. April 14, 1935, was called "Black Sunday."

TAKE A LOOK!

Take a look at the map below. In which states was erosion the worst?

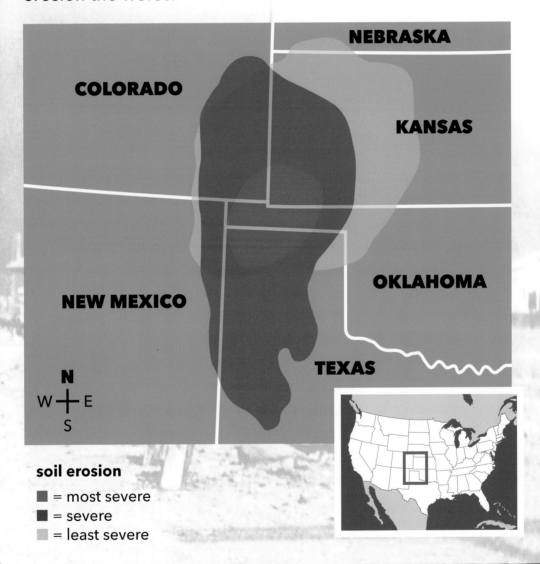

NEBRASKA

COLORADO

KANSAS

NEW MEXICO

OKLAHOMA

TEXAS

N
W ― E
S

soil erosion

■ = most severe
■ = severe
■ = least severe

CHAPTER 2
FARMERS ON THE MOVE

The drought and dust storms lasted nine years. People wore masks to cover their mouths and noses. Why? Breathing in the dust made people sick. Some even died.

dust mask

Without crops, farmers could not make money. They also could not feed their livestock. Many packed up and left.

Where did they go? Many went to places that weren't hit by the drought, like California. They became **migrant workers**. They picked crops for little money.

WHAT DO YOU THINK?

The U.S. government hired photographers during this time. Their photos appeared in popular magazines. They helped people in cities see what was happening. How does news spread now? Is it similar to or different from this time? How?

migrant worker

CHAPTER 3

END OF THE DUST BOWL

President Franklin D. Roosevelt helped. He started **conservation** projects. People were hired to plant trees. The trees helped block wind. Their roots held soil in place.

tree planting

New farming techniques helped, too. **Crop rotation** was one. Farmers rotated which crops they planted in each field. This kept the soil healthy.

irrigation
system

Irrigation systems helped, too. They brought water from rivers or underground to farmlands. This way, crops got water even if it didn't rain.

WHAT DO YOU THINK?

Starting in 1933, the U.S. government began buying large amounts of land. Why? So people couldn't farm it.  They also replanted grasses. This helped soil recover. Do you think the government should protect land? Why or why not?

Rain finally fell in the fall of 1939. Crops grew. The Dust Bowl ended. But the new ways of farming were here to stay. The U.S. government still helps farmers conserve soil today. They pay them not to farm certain fields. Many farmers use irrigation, too!

DID YOU KNOW?

Farmers grow foods we eat! Like what? Corn is the most popular crop. It is turned into foods like cereal. It feeds animals, too.

modern
irrigation system

QUICK FACTS & TOOLS

1939
Rains end the
nine-year drought.

1930
Drought begins
in the Great Plains.

MARCH 4, 1933
President Franklin D. Roosevelt takes
office. He helps the country out of the
Great Depression and the Dust Bowl.

APRIL 14, 1935
The worst dust storm occurs.
Scientists estimate that as
much as 300 million tons
(272 million metric tons)
of topsoil blew away on
this day. People call this
day Black Sunday.

1932
Fourteen dust
storms occur.

1933
Thirty-eight dust storms
occur. The first soil erosion
camp opens to help control
dust storms.

MARCH 1937
The Civilian Conservation
Corps begins planting trees
on the Great Plains.

1931
Dust storms first hit
the Great Plains.

MAY 1934
The dust storms spread from
the Dust Bowl area. By this time,
about 75 percent of the country
and 27 states are affected.

conservation: The protection of valuable things, especially forests, wildlife, natural resources, and artistic or historic objects.

crop rotation: The practice of growing different crops on the same land to preserve the productivity of the soil.

crops: Plants grown for food.

drought: A period of very little rainfall.

erode: To wear away gradually by wind or water.

Great Depression: A period of time in the 1930s when the United States and many other countries were in a very bad economic downturn.

Great Plains: A large, flat area of the central United States and western Canada that is covered in grasslands.

irrigation: The process of supplying water to crops by artificial means, such as channels and pipes.

livestock: Animals that are kept or raised on a farm or ranch.

migrant workers: People who move from one area or country to another in search of work.

plowed: Broke up soil using a piece of farm equipment pulled by an animal or tractor.

INDEX

Black Sunday 10

California 14

conservation 16, 20

crop rotation 17

crops 6, 9, 13, 14, 17, 19, 20

drought 9, 12, 14

dust storm 4, 5, 10, 12

erode 9, 11

farmers 6, 13, 17, 20

grasslands 6

Great Depression 6

Great Plains 4, 5, 6, 9

irrigation 19, 20

livestock 6, 13

migrant workers 14

Oklahoma 4

photographers 14

Roosevelt, Franklin D. 16

roots 9, 16

soil 6, 9, 11, 16, 17, 19, 20

trees 16

U.S. government 14, 19, 20

TO LEARN MORE

Finding more information is as easy as 1, 2, 3.

❶ Go to www.factsurfer.com

❷ Enter "DustBowl" into the search box.

❸ Choose your book to see a list of websites.

FACT SURFER